Cheerful Devotions to Give

Amy Bolding

BAKER BOOK HOUSE
Grand Rapids, Michigan 49506

ISBN: 0-8010-0868-9

First printing, December 1984
Second printing, June 1985
Third printing, November 1986
Fourth printing, June 1988

Printed in the United States of America

Contents

Special Days

1
Your Gifts

Blessed be the Lord, who daily loadeth us with benefits, even the God of our salvation (Ps. 68:19).

Yesterday a letter came from a young woman we knew from her early childhood. When she was nine, her mother died. When she was a teen, her only brother was killed in an automobile accident. But she went on with her life, and by the sheer force of stubborn will, she worked her way through nurses' training.

She did find some happiness, however, as an earlier letter from her reflected. She had married and found a good job. She and her husband were in the process of adopting a baby. All seemed well.

But this letter was sad. The adoption didn't go through. The natural mother of the child had asked for her baby, and the judge granted the request. Then, her husband pressed for divorce. She had no choice but to let him go. In this letter she concluded: "What is left?"

I answered by pointing out the gifts she still had. She was young enough to have a child of her own should she remarry. She had a good job. She was a consecrated Christian.

If your whole world seemed to fall apart suddenly, would you be able to count the many gifts and blessings you pos-

sessed? Through life's testings and trials, God does not withdraw his gifts from us. Jesus said, "Come unto me all ye that
labor and are heavy laden, and I will give you rest" (Matt.
11:28).

As a child of God you have the greatest gifts of all: God's
love and comfort. And you can better experience these gifts by
adopting this little motto: "Go down the road looking for
Jesus." You will see Jesus in the beauty of the earth, in the
smile of a child, or in the kind word from a friend. You can
find Jesus during the quiet moments while you're reading the
Bible.

God's love and comfort become more real to us through
another gift—the privilege of prayer. What a great gift prayer
is! And it's free to all God's children. Through prayer we receive
God's power.

A man decided to cook breakfast to surprise his wife on her
birthday. As he started preparing, he put the coffee and then
the water in the percolator and left it standing on the cabinet
where he saw his wife leave it. After he fried the eggs and
bacon and buttered the toast, something didn't seem right.
The familiar sound of the percolator "pop-popping" was missing. What went wrong? He had forgotten to plug in the cord.
The percolator had no power.

You, too, must stay plugged into God's power by prayer. No
prayer means little power. Prayer connects you to the power-
line through which God's love surges into your soul.

Along with the gift of our Savior's care when you are heavy
laden, you possess the free gift of salvation. No person or
circumstance can take this gift away from you. How wonderful
it is to appreciate and receive these gifts by praying to God in
the name of Christ. And through God's wisdom, and not your
whims, your prayers are answered.

Then, you have the gift of Christian friends, who will pray with you and for you. When David thought he had no friends left, Jonathan, the king's son, remained a true friend. Remember the story of Ruth and Naomi? Naomi lost her husband and two sons. Alone and helpless, she took the long trek across the wilderness to her native land. But one of her daughters-in-law, Ruth—true friend that she was—went with her. Later, Ruth gleaned in the field to get grain for the two of them. Such friendships as these (and you must *be* a friend) reflect our relationship with Christ. Jesus said: "By this shall all men know that ye are my disciples, if ye have love one to another" (John 13:35).

You also possess the gift of ideas. You can think and plan what you want to do with your life. What a wonderful blessing your mind is! Some people do not share the mental health that you enjoy. They do not share a normal capacity to think creatively. In many circumstances of life they must be told what to do. Thank God for a sound mind! Do you consider your ideas as a wonderful gift from God? As a senior citizen, I have lessening ability and zip to carry out my plans and ideas. But I keep my "percolator of prayer" plugged in. I still can rejoice in the ability to use my mind.

Another gift is the inner wealth of feeling at peace with God. One pastor shared how he determined to perform an act of kindness every day for someone other than his own family or church members. But soon he nearly forsook his resolve. A church in another city had invited him to be one of their featured speakers. The plane on which he came was late, and he felt that he would have to rush to get to the church on time. But an elderly woman sitting next to him told him, as the plane landed, how much she needed a ride from the airport to her home—across town. A thought tempted him: "See what trouble you can get into when you try to be a servant?" But he decided to stick by his resolution. He drove her to her door and carried her luggage inside. Although he would be late at the church, he felt good about it. The people at the service graciously waited until he arrived. He had served someone in need, and felt at peace with God.

You may have special gifts to make others happy. My oldest daughter is a very good cook. She is often called on to cook something for parties or for church meetings. Not long ago we visited her. Her kitchen counters were full because she had been baking all morning. She made brownies for a men's group her husband was going to attend, a lovely cake for a youth group her teenage daughter was going to, and two gallons of punch for a bridal shower for which she was the hostess. Added to all of that, her pastor's two little children were there under her care so he and his wife could run into town to make an important hospital call. She used her expertise in the kitchen to touch many lives outside her own home. Consider what you do well and how you are using your gifts to make the lives of others happier.

Here's another gift. If you enjoy good health, think of this as a gift from God. Far too often, we take that gift for granted. We reach for false comfort too often by magnifying our aches and pains.

Take a good look at the gifts you have right now. Erase self-pity for the bumps and disappointments you experienced in the past. If you have joy and gladness today, give these to your family and your friends. Communicate God's blessings and love.

"Acknowledge Him in all thy ways, and He shall direct thy paths" (Prov. 3:6).

I ask not, God,
That I be great
In what this world can give;
I only ask
That Thy great love
Shall guide the life I live

Unknown

Gifts

Around you, unkindness and chaos abound;
    The mean and the ugly are near,
Much sickness and sorrow may always be found,
    And there's often abundance of fear.

So in this wide ocean of crisis and crime,
    Try to be an island of joy;
Just cheer up your spot as you clean out the grime
    And skip the old yen to destroy.

More islands of peace and assurance would fill
    The needs of those hurting today.
Will you be one, please; yes, you can, if you will,
    And bless those around you, I pray.

J. T. Bolding

2
The Touch of a Hand

How shall we escape, if we neglect so great salvation (Heb. 2:3).

And they shall be mine, saith the Lord of hosts, in that day when I make up my jewels; and I will spare them as a man spareth his own son that serveth him (Mal. 3:17).

The poet William Cowper long ago wrote the lines:

> God works in a mysterious way
> His wonders to perform.
> He plants His footsteps on the sea
> And rides upon the storm.

One time when my road seemed very rough, a friend placed a hand on my shoulder and said a kind word. I gained courage and went on. Soon the road seemed smoother.

During World War II, I was left alone with my three small children while my husband went overseas to serve as a chaplain. Another young woman in the town where I lived was kind to me, and we had a lot in common. Her husband was also overseas. In spite of our friendship, I kept feeling lonelier and more sorry for myself.

When I thought I could go no further, she received a telegram telling her that her husband had been killed in battle.

As I hurried to her to place a hand on her shoulder in love and sympathy, it was clear to me that other loads were heavier than mine.

Never neglect the opportunity to reach out your hand to touch someone in need. That was Jesus' way with others. Bread lasts but a day, but the touch of a hand will live on. A loving touch may be an important way to witness for Jesus. "How shall we escape, if we neglect so great salvation?"

A few years ago, some new houses were built on our block. As people moved in I thought I would go and get acquainted with them. One of the women, three doors up the street, was friendly. I invited her to come to our church. But she was not interested, although her membership was in a church fifty miles away.

Year after year I watched that family. The little boy grew up large enough to mow lawns, and I hired him to take care of our lawn. The family bought a camper, motorcycles, and a boat. Everything seemed geared for a life of pleasure. But we neglected to reach out a hand to that family again to invite them to church.

On a hot summer day two ladies came to my door. They were from a church all the way across town. They were getting names of children who might ride a bus to their church. Then we noticed a big bus coming down our street while we were eating our Sunday lunch.

One day, as my husband was puttering in the flower bed, the man from up the street came to visit with him. He asked whether we still needed his son to mow our grass. Then, he told what he really came to tell.

His two children had been riding the bus we saw each Sunday. They had been converted a few weeks back. He and his wife had gone to see them baptized and had also joined.

We were so happy for them and for the little church across town. But we were saddened that we had not reached out our hand again to them. We missed the blessing that just a little more effort might have brought.

One of our friends belonged to a large church in Dallas. He would always try to get to the pastor and shake his hand. Something made him long for that small personal contact.

His wife told me his story. His mother died when he was very young and his father placed him in a private institution. When he reached the age of fifteen he was told his father had died and his stepmother would no longer pay his fees. At fifteen, he was thrown out on the world. He worked at many jobs just to stay alive. How he longed for someone to touch him with love, to encourage him in his struggle for survival. The touch of the pastor's hand meant a great deal to him, even though now he was financially successful in life and had a happy marriage.

Dr. R. G. Lee, a famous Baptist preacher, believed strongly in reaching out a hand to those in need. When young people came to his study he took time to counsel with them. Often he helped them through cash loans or gifts. Before any young person left, he prayed with them. Only eternity will reveal how much good was accomplished because Dr. Lee took time to touch the young lives in his church.

Sometimes taking time to touch the life of another doesn't seem worth the effort. We do not know why God impresses us to do certain things for certain people. But we do know that God will reveal all to us when we get to heaven.

Now, we may not always feel motivated to reach out. But our challenge is to obey Christ and reap the rich blessing by reaching out to help and encourage others.

A Man's Never Whipped
Until He's Whipped Inside

No matter what hardships or dangers assail,
And though health, wealth, friends, and everything fail,
A man can brave storms and conquer the tide;
For one's never whipped till he's whipped inside.

Though bruised and bleeding and cast to the ground,
He'll come up for more; you can't keep him down.
Though weakened and worn, his time will he bide;
A man's never whipped till he's whipped inside!

The score's against him, the crowd is all jeers;
He fights to the end and wins greater cheers.
He knows in his heart, though men praise or chide,
A man's never whipped till he's whipped inside!

Though enemies mock and friends may betray,
He'll last the long night and win the new day.
He holds to the truth all great men have tried;
A man's never whipped till he's whipped inside!

                                        Unknown

3

Heed God's Call! For Service Big or Small

Thou shalt delight thyself in the Lord; and I will cause thee to ride upon the high places of the earth, and feed thee with the heritage of Jacob thy father (Isa. 58:14).

Unto you, O men, I call; and my voice is to the sons of man. O ye simple understand wisdom: and, ye fools, be ye of an understanding heart (Prov. 8:4, 5).

The son of a wealthy farmer felt that God was calling him to be a missionary. Having some worldly goods of his own, he hastily went to another country, with his family, to be a missionary. He felt deeply that God wanted him to serve in a foreign land.

He soon discovered that without training in mission work, he was very ineffective. And, because of his tender heart he had given much of his money to beggers. Both his wife's parents and his own were sending him money to help feed his family.

After a while he met another missionary, one who was serving under a board. This convinced him to return to the United States and study missions in a seminary.

You see, God calls us, but He also knows what training we need. He allowed His own Son to be trained on earth for thirty years before the three years of intense, public ministry began.

14

Therefore, the young man and his wife went to school. They worked very hard and graduated. But God had still another lesson for him. He wanted this young man to learn patience.

When school was over and he finally held the coveted diploma in his hand, a church did not come rushing to call him. After a few months of frustration and much prayer, God called him to a little church. After two years as a pastor, he had an opportunity to meet with the foreign mission board and be sent to a mission field. God's timing was different and His plan was far better.

Leave Me Not!

Still let Thy wisdom be my guide,
Nor take Thy flight from me away;
Still with me let Thy grace abide,
That I from Thee may never stray.
Let Thy Word richly in me dwell,
Thy peace and love, my portion be;
My joy to endure and do Thy will.
Till perfect I am found in Thee.

John Wesley

When Wesley wrote these words, he had no idea of the many wonderful things God was calling him to accomplish. He only knew that he wanted to serve.

Our scripture verse at the beginning of this meditation tells us God will do great things for those who heed His call. The next verses tell us that the simple can understand wisdom, and even the foolish can have understanding hearts. So we as Christians are to heed God's call, for He does call each Christian for some service.

Christ told the story of a master who entrusted different amounts of money to three servants. The two who worked and multiplied their money were richly rewarded, but the one who buried his money was punished.

After we heed God's call, we are to prepare for service. We are to pray for guidance. We are to be brave and have faith to follow our Lord as He calls. Christian service is what we allow Christ to do through us. And God is greater than all our difficulties.

We also must answer callings to the smaller tasks of life. During the first few years I was a pastor's wife, I was scared. I thought I had to please all the people, but I soon found that they all had different ideas about what I should wear, cook, or say.

And, at our first church, I recognized that some members taught better than I did, sang better than I could, and were better looking than I was. But they couldn't out-smile me. I had something to smile about. God had answered my prayers. The war was over and my husband was home safe. That he was pastor of a nice church also made me happy.

Each Sunday I smiled and spoke to as many as I could. Some people had heavy hearts. They had loved ones who were injured or who died while serving their country. They needed a smile.

In our next church God let me grow some. I taught a class and served in other ways. Some place I read the following statement: It isn't your position that makes you happy or unhappy. It is your disposition."

As God's children who try to heed His call, we may identify with the little boy who was asked, "Can you read?" He responded, "I can read numbers but I can't read reading."

"What do you mean?"

"Well, see those signs on the highway?"

"Yes."

"Well, I can read how far, but I can't read where to."

Concerning your life God knows how far, and He knows where to. You are but to pray and listen and follow.

With God's grace, try to go as far as you can to use your gifts to fulfill your calling. Only God knows where He will lead us. Our destinies on earth may be beyond our expectations!

Handicaps

I have so many handicaps
  And most of them I placed on me:
I am afraid to undertake
  To fill the many needs I see.

And then I haven't time, you know,
  To do those little extra things,
For I am such a busy one;
  My time just flies on racing wings.

I am too tired; I don't know how;
  And then someone I might offend;
I'm not a specialist, you see,
  For I do well to just attend.

And so I use some old excuse,
  And very rarely warm a pew;
There is so very, very much
  My handicaps won't let me do.

J. T. Bolding

4

Windows in Dark Places

Now when Daniel knew that the writing was signed, he went into his house; and his windows being open in his chamber toward Jerusalem, he kneeled upon his knees three times a day, and prayed, and gave thanks before his God, as he did aforetime (Dan. 6:10).

. . . and the windows of heaven were opened (Gen. 9:11).

. . . the windows of heaven (Mal. 3:10).

The other morning I felt grumpy. Perhaps it was from my dreary bedroom. I left the room and went to the front part of the house. The shades were up and the sun was bright and beautiful. How much better I felt! I went back to the bedroom and opened the drapes. My disposition became sunny as well.

Each day, if we get away from home at all, we are apt to meet someone who needs a window opened in a dark heart and life. Once we were visiting in a hospital room. The patient started complaining about what a bad day it was. My husband, who was near the window, quietly pulled the cord on the venetian blind. The room quickly brightened and the view of a lovely lake met our eyes. The patient began to smile.

Windows are mentioned a number of times in the Bible. The verse in Genesis is talking about the windows of heaven.

In Malachi 3:10, God promises that he will open the windows of heaven and pour out blessings upon us, if we do what He commands.

One Sunday I overheard a woman say to another: "I don't like that blouse with the skirt you are wearing." That loud mouth closed a window for her friend and made her day dark.

On another day I met a friend on the street. I felt windblown and hurried. As we talked a moment, she said in leaving, "Amy, it always makes my day when I see you." Needless to say she made my day! I went about my tasks with a light heart, and hoped I passed my joy to others I met. We have the choice of opening windows in dark places.

There are numbers of ways to open windows for others as well as for ourselves. My husband and I went to the opening of a new Savings and Loan Company. It was one of those days in West Texas when the morning starts out cold but then turns very hot and windy.

I dressed in a wool suit and felt comfortable. At the opening, however, I was the only woman there with white hair. And, I was the only one wearing a wool suit. I felt out of place. But as we stood around visiting, a tall man spoke to us. He was a friend from years past.

"I am so glad to see both of you; you look so good. Are you happy in retirement?"

He opened happy windows for us. I forgot that the day had turned hot. I simply rejoiced to see this friend again.

I made up my mind that I would go about opening windows of encouragement for others. I would stop thinking only of myself and give myself away to others.

When a missionary was asked why she chose to spend her life in a foreign land, this was her reply: "I have but one candle of life to burn, and would rather burn it out where people are dying in darkness, than in a land which is flooded with lights."

If God lives in you, then your actions will be Christlike because it is in your nature.

A poor man reared three sons. After the boys reached manhood, he gave each of them a coin and homemade candle. He called them in and gave them this advice: "Try to find work to feed yourself and save your coin for a rainy day. Your candle represents your candle of life. Never burn it except for a good cause."

The middle boy was only eighteen when he left home. He found a lot of places where he could work to meet his simple needs. He was tired at night and went to bed early. He did not need to burn his candle.

One night he heard a child crying. He got up from his resting place, took his candle, and lighted it. He found a mother with a sick child trying to find the way to a doctor. With the bright light from his candle he soon led her to the physician.

On another night, he heard a knock on his door. It was a lost child. Soon, he helped the child to reach home by light of the candle. During other nights he was called on to help some person in distress by using his candle.

Then he thought of something. Since he remembered how his father made candles, he would teach the people in the village how to make candles for themselves. Soon, all the windows of the village had lighted candles in them each evening. His heart was happy and full. He had helped others.

Each person in the world has been given one candle of life by our heavenly Father. How are you using yours? Are you lighting the dark windows in the people around you?

Not only do we need to put our own lights in the dark windows of other lives, we also need to think of famous people who have lighted the windows of our nation.

George Washington led in the fight for freedom for our nation. But our nation did not become totally free. Later, Abraham Lincoln lighted the windows of thousands of lives as he freed the slaves in America. Charles A. Lindbergh led the way for modern aviation as he made the first solo flight across the ocean in a plane.

Many great educators could be mentioned who made our nation the most enlightened one in the world today. Great men of all types and backgrounds have walked life's pathways and left the world a brighter place because they lived and because they cared.

You may not be called to be a great leader. But the hope and joy you light in the hearts of others will prompt them to be a blessing to others. People are hungry for things that light up their lives.

Here's a statement I like very much:

> I live in a very small house
> but
> my windows open on a very
> large world.

When a school was built on his reservation, a Navajo Indian said: "A new fresh wind is blowing across the reservation; it is the wind of change." You bring a wind of change to people when you light their dark windows with a kind word or deed.

Open a Window

Open a window for someone you know;
  Let the light shine on his sad, gloomy day;
Muster a smile that will let your love show,
  And you will brighten his difficult way.

Open a window and let the light in,
  So he may see God's good blessings galore,
And be inspired in his battle to win,
  So he will draw from God's bountiful store.

Open a window and get the great joy
  Which will come when you help those in need;
Get down to work and stop being so coy,
  As you match your good word with a deed.

J. T. Bolding

5
Life Is Not a Trifle!

Fear ye not therefore, ye are of more value than many sparrows (Matt. 10:31).

For he shall be as a tree planted by the waters, and that spreadeth out her roots by the river . . . (Jer. 17:8).

Life is a precious gift from God. We should treat it as a divine gift.

On my dressing table and in my jewelry box I have many pieces of costume jewelry. They are trifles; I like them, but I do not treasure them. On the other hand, in a safety deposit box at the bank, I have some valuable pieces of jewelry that I treasure.

People treat life like I treat my jewelry. Some young people—by drinking, gambling, or taking dope—throw away the gift of life as if it were just a trifle. In contrast, other young people strive to make good grades in school. They are ambitious to make their lives count for something in the world. To them, life is a treasure.

In the scripture above we are told how God values us. In a number of places in the Bible, man is described as a tree. The tree is strong in the face of drought or storm. The tree brings forth fruit. The tree provides shade for other creatures. The psalmist (1:3) describes a righteous man as one who prospers like a healthy tree.

You may plant your life by the river's bank
Where the limpid waters flow:
You may plant your life in the shaded glen,
Where no chilling tempests blow:
You may plant your life on the mountain's height,
'Neath the smile of the arching blue:
You may plant your life where you will, my friend,
Since the choice is left to you,
But if I am to choose the course of my life,
As the fields of the world I behold,
I will plant my life in the heart of the young
To bear ten-thousand fold.

Unknown

Since God values us, we should value our own lives. Children
have to be taught the value of life and how to be careful of
danger. One of our favorite family pictures is of our oldest
granddaughter when she was three years old. She had found
the kitchen empty and climbed up on the cabinet. She managed to get the cabinet door open and then spotted bananas
on a plate. When her grandfather discovered her, he hurried to
get the camera. The snapshot recorded her precarious position.
One tiny hand held tightly to the side of the cabinet; the other
hand reached for a banana. She had achieved her aim to climb
on the cabinet. But when she finally looked down, she became
aware of her danger.

Our granddaughter's adventure was prompted by a child's
native curiosity. But she was told that what she did was
dangerous. Responsibility and decision-making must be taught
during these early years nonetheless.

If we would treat our lives with the respect they deserve, we
must learn to make decisions. We must learn to ask ourselves;
"Is it right both now and in the long run?"

How sad when young people fail to acquire moral judgement. Recently two boys, in our town, went up and down the street shooting out the windows of parked cars with their B.B. guns. A young couple sitting in a car in a driveway spotted the vandals. They slipped in the house and called the police. In a matter of moments the police were there and apprehended the boys. These boys didn't think about or didn't care about what was right or wrong. Repair shops estimated hundreds of dollars of damages for each car. These boys were trifling with their lives. They must live with a bad mark on their records. Nonetheless, parents of the vandals excused them: "Boys will be boys."

Boys will be good boys only if their parents demand that they be good. We trifle with life when wrong behavior is excused.

We can better value our lives by carrying out assignments of small tasks. Each minor accomplishment may lead to greater opportunity.

One of our former paperboys took the time to place the newspaper in a convenient place by the door for an older woman. Although this was not much trouble actually, most boys would have said, "I haven't time for that."

On one pleasant day, the elderly lady was sitting on her porch. When her paperboy came by she asked him to write down his name and address.

Three years later, this boy finished high school and was looking for a job to help pay his way through college. He applied at the largest department store in town. Later he was invited into the owner's office.

The owner arose, reached across the desk, and shook his hand. "You have a job here as long as you need it. You were my mother's paperboy, and you brought her joy by always putting her paper where she could reach it."

"That was just my duty, Sir," he replied.

"Duty or not, you were the first paperboy who cared. You have a job with me as long as you want it."

Therefore we exhibit the importance of our own lives by treating other people as if they were important.

I was impressed with a prominent athlete who advised young people, "Stay in school and be cool." He was a champion in his field, but his heart was set on helping young people to build better lives.

Normally, parents sacrifice much to get medical help for a sick child. Physical life is very precious. Some of those same parents, however, fail to be concerned about the moral and spiritual life of their children. They fail to make certain that their children learn to trust Christ for eternal life. They will take off from work to bring their sick child to the doctor, but they find it too much trouble to see that their children are in Sunday school and church each week.

We are precious and important to God. He gave each of us our lives and the lives of our children to influence and control. He has given each of us the kingdom of the mind and heart. However that kingdom is ruled—well or poorly—so will the life go.

A senior evangelist, reading the morning paper after he had preached the night before, noticed a reference to himself as an aging preacher. He was shocked that anyone would consider him old. He still felt young at heart and enthusiastic. He felt life was still out there before him with more tasks to accomplish for the Lord. If we don't trifle with life from the start we'll have much to treasure during our later years.

Life is a scrap-book, torn and old
In which our little lives are told—
And when the twilight shadows fall
This is the sweetest thing of all;
To turn the pages of the years,
Remembering—with happy tears—
The faithful love, the perfect friend.
These things are treasured to the end.

                              Unknown

6
The "Maybe" of Life

*. . . it may be that the Lord will work for us: for there is no
restraint to the Lord to save by many or by few* (1 Sam. 14:6).

The fourteenth chapter of First Samuel tells the
story of Jonathan and his servant. They prayed that God would
give them a sign about a battle. Then they climbed up to a
Philistine outpost, where the two of them routed and killed
twenty Philistine soldiers. The rest of the Philistines panicked,
and were easily chased by the army of Israel.

That day these two men helped to save the people of Israel
from their Philistine enemies. The point of the chapter is that
God does not require a host of people to begin a battle. God
can accomplish much through just a few who courageously
act and place their trust in Him.

Remember Gideon? He started out with an army of thirty-
two thousand. By God's tests, however, he reduced his army to
three hundred. The battle was won with a few.

We cannot live our lives on what may be. We have to make
decisions, after we have prayed about them, and abide by them.
Both Jonathan and Gideon asked for God's will in their decision.

The friendships we make often determine the way we go in
life. Don't choose your friends on a "maybe" basis. Ask for

God's guidance. Many young people have picked the wrong friends and have been led into a life of sin. Many businessmen have trusted the financial advice of careless friends and lost their life savings.

What if Jonathan and his servant had started out after saying; "Let's go now, we haven't time to talk to God." Maybe God will be with you when you go on an adventure, but don't dare venture out without asking for His guidance.

Two boys from the plains of Texas decided to go to the mountains of New Mexico for a weekend. They parked their car near a ski lodge. Then they strapped on their packs and started the hike.

When they did not report to their homes or to work after the weekend, an alarm was sounded. Search parties went out to look for the young men. Five days later they heard a weak voice call: "Are you looking for me?" One was exhausted, his feet and hands frostbitten. The other had frozen to death.

If only they had stopped to talk to a forest ranger, he could have advised them that a storm was coming. He could have warned them that their packs and clothes were not adequate.

"It *may be* that the Lord will work for us." He will if we consult Him. The Lord is eager to work for His children. He waits for us to ask His advice. Life is full of "maybes" from birth to death. We take our chances on people, on things, on dangers, on friends, or on foes.

The one who does the most in God's great world is the one who does the most in his own little world. Often we say, "Maybe we will find God's will," or "Maybe we will go out and accomplish something significant." But it is no strain on God's resources for Him to give you what you need. God is an all-powerful God, not a "maybe" God.

Economically, 1928 was a very hard year for our family. I remember wanting a class ring very much. It seemed that I was the only one in my graduating class who had not ordered one. Finally, just before the deadline, I asked my father if he would buy a ring for me.

"Why, yes. You must have a class ring." He simply had not known it was time to order rings. And I was too afraid to ask for it earlier.

We miss many blessings because we are too timid to ask God for them. He has all the blessings to give, unlike my father who was struggling to feed his large family. God loves us and will bless us, even if we go to him with a "maybe" proposition.

Life has lots of "maybes" in it. But to live the best life possible we need to develop a feeling of personal responsibility.

A twelve-year-old farm boy was left alone at home one Saturday to watch over the farm. After his family had been gone for some time, a strong gusty wind came up. The boy put on his cap and went out to see if all was well. He saw that the wind had blown down an old wood gate to the barnyard. In the barnyard were several new calves. He knew they must be kept in at all costs. His attitude was: It is my responsibility to keep them safe until my dad gets home. He tried to pick up the gate but it was too heavy. Finding a long stick, the boy stood in place of the gate and kept the calves from getting out.

At last the long afternoon passed and the family returned.

"You did a fine thing, son. We could not afford to loose those calves." The father praised his sense of responsibility.

What if the boy had said; "Maybe the calves won't see that the gate is down. I don't want to stay out in the wind."

Some people fail to advance in their work because they are negative "maybe" people. Maybe I will not succeed. Maybe people will laugh at me. Maybe this is not the right time to act. Intimidated by these "maybe" statements, they find little or no advancement. Rather, like Jonathan and his servant, look only for the positive "maybes." It *may be* that the Lord will work for us." You can do it with God's help.

Days

The days so quickly come and go,
    Your precious youth will soon be spent;
'Twill slip away before you know,
    Therefore, be wise and diligent.

That when life's afternoon turns grey,
    And harvest comes for wild oats sown,
Your sad regret won't try to say,
    I'd have been better if I'd known.

Perk up my dear, my precious, friend,
    And be your very best today
That your tomorrow may not end
    In vain regret and sad dismay.

J. T. Bolding

7
Shopping Spree

Buy the truth and sell it not; also wisdom, and instruction, and understanding (Prov. 23:23).

During the first year after my husband retired, he could not get enough shopping. It was not that we needed much, but he had been working all his life, and shopping was a new experience. Of course it was not new to me. I had been shopping for my family for years.

Many days we would go shopping just to have some place to go. One year, we had all our Christmas gifts bought by August. We shopped so much for groceries that we had stored some canned goods in the garage. We loved running about town together to the advertised sales. It was as much fun to us as travel to far places is to some other retired people.

A guest preacher in our church mentioned that at least one-third of the world's population never went shopping in their life. As he spoke, I saw in my mind's eye the starving people we had seen on the television. Thousand of children and mothers with nothing except a few bowls of rice to eat. Silently I thanked God for His great blessing to America.

He went on to say that at least a third or more of the world's population had never slept on a bed. Soon we stopped most of our shopping sprees and started "shopping" for things to do that were more worthwhile. We spent much more time visiting hospitals and helping the sick.

The Things that Count

Not what we have—but what we use!
Not what we see—but what we choose—
These are the things that mar or bless
The sum of human happiness.
The things nearby, not things afar,
Not what we seem, but what we are.
These are the things that make or break,
That give the heart its joy or ache.
Not what seems fair, but what is true,
Not what we dream, but the good we do.
These are the things that shine like gems,
Like stars, in heaven's diadems.
Not as we take, but as we give,
Not as we pray, but as we live—
These are the things that make for peace
Both now and after time shall cease.

Chinese sayings, Source unknown

The writer of Proverbs (23:23) advised us to buy truth and sell it not; and also buy wisdom, instruction, and understanding. If we would shop for the things in this Scripture verse every day, we could avoid so many pitfalls in life.

Shopping

When wife goes window shopping,
    I sometimes tag along;
She really keeps me hopping,
    Though she's not very strong.

> She looks at things both pink and blue,
> 　　She goes for lace and frills,
> And mostly all I have to do
> 　　Is merely pay the bills.
>
> Now when we come to living,
> 　　To choosing friends and such,
> We need to plan on giving,
> 　　Not how to get so much.
>
> 　　　　　　　　　　J. T. Bolding

About the time we grew tired of going shopping just to have an excuse to get out of the house, my sister gave us a copy of a new version of the Bible. For some time we had been using the King James version and had read it through, two chapters a day, at the breakfast table. So we took our new Bible and started reading two chapters of it each day. Sometimes we would not agree with what we read and would look at the same verse in the King James.

We also read *The Living Bible* in the same way. It was so much fun to read and compare. Now we are almost through the *Criswell Study Bible* and have on hand a copy of the *New International Version*. We discovered that these daily shopping trips in the Scriptures are very exciting.

A lady sat down on a train by a one-legged man. She stood it as long as she could, and then said: "Please tell me what happened to your leg?"

"I will if you will not ask another question."

"I promise I will not ask." She replied. "Tell me!"

"My leg was bitten off."

Some of the stories in the Bible are like that; they make us want to dig out the answers. When Bible stories prompt questions we read on.

Shopping to find new friends is a very important task. When my husband retired we had a lot more time on our hands than we had ever known before. I assumed that our friends in the church and on the church staff would continue to invite us to their social gatherings. I soon realized that we had been included many times because of the position my husband held for sixteen years as associate pastor. Now, the new worker took our place. But other retired people began asking us to their homes. We returned the invitation and soon we had some lovely new friends.

Shopping for friends is a serious task for children, teenagers, and young married people as well. My married grandson and his wife moved to another town. They had been taught to develop new friendships in new situations.

The first church they attended had very few young married people. So they tried another, with success! They were invited to after-church fellowships and they invited couples to their house. Soon they were happy in this town because of their new friends.

The right friends are vitally important. A foreign missionary, home on furlough, was speaking to a large audience. "I feel at home with you although I do not know your names. I know you worship my Lord." If we shop for friends who worship our Lord, we will have the right kind of friends.

Give a Hand

It's easy to smile at another's mistakes,
   Or cry when it's we who fall down,
It's fun to enjoy that which someone else bakes,
   Or act the ridiculous clown.

But giving a hand to help a mistake,
      And wiping away a sad frown,
Encourages friends and may offer a break
      When hope for them may have left town.

Just whistle a tune, sing a bright cheery song,
      Reach out your own hand as you run;
Yes, give of yourself to help right some foul wrong
      And blessed you shall be when the day is done.

J. T. Bolding

8
Partnership of Happiness

Let your conversation be without covetousness; and be content with such things as ye have; for he hath said, I will never leave thee, nor forsake thee   (Heb. 13:5).

A partnership in happiness needs at least two people of the same mind. Often we see two young people of the same mind. They may fall in love and get married. Their continued happiness, however, depends on their staying of the same mind.

If they have the same mind about the value of money, they will agree about purchases and work for a common goal financially. If they have been taught good manners as children, they will be better equipped to keep harmony in their marriage. On and on we could go about harmony and the partnership of happiness. The greatest need for happiness in a partnership is for both to be strong Christians—devout followers of God.

A woman over seventy-years-old and married more than fifty years said: "I have been well contented all my life and happy most of the time." Too many young people today are taking the attitude, "If our marriage doesn't work, we can break up." But anyone who wants a partnership of happiness must take the attitude, "I'll be content, whatever comes."

37

The last part of Luke 3:14 admonishes: "Be content with your wages." The philosopher Goethe wrote out some rules for a happy partnership with others:

Health enough to make work a pleasure. Wealth enough to support your needs. Strength to battle with difficulties and overcome them.

Grace enough to confess your sins and forsake them. Patience enough to toil until some good is accomplished. Charity enough to see some good in your neighbor.

Love enough to move you to be useful and helpful to others. Faith enough to make real the things of God.

Hope enough to remove all anxious fears concerning the future.

In war time many soldiers have buddies. They are close to each other in their loneliness. They help each other to combat the fears and disappointments of being away from their loved ones and homes. A man who worked for many years in the composing room of the newspaper at Cambridge, Massachusetts, placed an ad in the paper in memory of his buddy during World War II. The ad read:

In Memorial to a buddy who helped storm Omaha Beach, Normandy, June 6, 1944. No greater love hath a man than this: That he lay down his life for his friend.

The friend had been killed as he carried Frank Rogan to safety after he was wounded. Frank Rogan was happy to be alive and wanted to do something to show the world how much he appreciated his friend and buddy for saving his life. That was a partnership of love and sacrifice.

Partnerships in happiness are vital to our well being. Most of us enjoy having someone with whom we can share our joys and someone who will rejoice with us. In the beginning God said, "It is not good for man to be alone." Each day we should wake with the thought: Let me give a little of myself today to make the world a brighter place.

For a while we took an eight-year-old boy to Sunday school with us. One Sunday when we were driving home our young friend said: "You sure are lucky."

"Why?" my husband asked.

"So many people speak to you."

A blessing we had taken for granted was greatly desired by a small boy. We were sad when his family moved away and he could not go with us to church anymore.

Nan broke her hip. Since she had no close relatives she had to be sent to a nursing home. There she saw a man who was all twisted with disease and was also blind. Her heart was touched deeply, and she prayed about his plight. The Lord healed Nan. She became the eyes, hands, and feet for the man she had prayed about. For eleven years she tried to be for him a partner in happiness.

Circumstances of life sometimes are adverse, and we become discouraged. But if God is our partner in happiness, we will be able to weather the storms and be content.

We should be content always, if we have given God our hearts. We know that we have the absolute assurance of God's love. The Bible tells us over and over that God loves His children.

A requirement for happiness is that we love each other. The Bible says: "We know that we have passed from death unto life, because we love the brethren" (I John 3:14). Ben Franklin said: "I early found that when I worked for myself alone, myself alone worked for me; but when I worked also for others, others worked also for me.

May I share one of the sweetest stories I ever heard about a partnership in love?

A teenage boy was the star batter on his school baseball team. His father attended every game and was very loyal to his son's team. Then the father died just a few days before a big game. The teammates expected their star to be absent. He was, however, not only present but he also played the best game he had ever played.

A friend asked him why he came to play when his father had just died. With a sad but confident smile, he replied: "You see my father was blind, and yet he came to support me. Today he is in heaven, and this is the first time he has seen me play. I did my best for him."

The Bible says "Thou shalt love thy neighbor as thyself" (Matt. 19:9). This means we must care about all of our neighbors, not just the ones who bring us gifts from their garden or kitchen.

A woman in Dallas was left with an afflicted child to support. After she found the best job she could, she then supplemented her income by having a "garage sale" once in a while.

During one of these sales, a neighbor called the police to come and see what was going on. After the police had apologized for coming to her garage sale, the irate mother went across to their neighbor's house.

"I am trying in every way I can to support my son, and keep a home for him. If you will just let me alone, I will never bother you."

"I was thinking of the good of the community."

"Well, you might remember people live in the community, and they have to eat and pay taxes the same as you do."

After that, the two women never spoke to each other. How much they both missed by not following the practice of loving your neighbor as yourself.

9

Down Payment on a Dream

Let the king tell his servants the dream, and we will shew the interpretation of it. The king answered and said, I know of certainty that ye would gain the time, because ye see the thing is gone from me (Dan. 2:7, 8)

In the second chapter of the Book of Daniel is the story of King Nebuchadnezzar's dream. He could not remember the dream, and none of the wise men of his court in Babylon could tell him what his dream had been.

But Daniel told the king that he would reveal and interpret the dream if he could have a little time. Daniel and his three fellow captives prayed, and God revealed the dream to Daniel in a night vision. When he told the king what his dream had been and what it meant, Daniel was rewarded.

We experience dreams in the night. But we can also consciously dream through our aspirations and ambitions. Children dream of growing up. Parents dream of educating their children. Grandparents dream of leisure, travel, and comfort.

But we must not forget a segment of society that has no more dreams. The very old who have been placed in nursing homes and forgotten have little or nothing to look forward to; they have no more dreams left. What are we doing to make their remaining days on earth more meaningful and cheerful?

It is good to dream and to plan. One man we know dreamed that each of his ten grandchildren would be able to purchase a home. He gave each a sizeable amount of money to help make his dream come true.

One by one the four older grandchildren took their money, added to it, and made a down payment on a home. Each of the younger grandchildren, as they received their gift, placed the money in savings accounts, to withdraw the funds when they were grown. The grandchildren shared the dream of spending the money purchasing their homes. Grandfather felt well rewarded and pleased as his dream was being fulfilled.

What about people who lose their dreams—whose hopes are dashed through harsh circumstances? A minister and his wife were returning home from a religious retreat. A sudden, hard rainstorm blurred the visibility, so they pulled off to the side of the road to wait out the downpour. Both leaned back to take a nap.

Suddenly another car hit them from the rear. Fortunately, they were not hurt, but the man who ran into them was injured seriously. He was rushed to the nearest town with a hospital. As the minister and his wife stayed to see that he had proper attention, they heard his sad story.

The injured man was married and the father of two small children. He had lost his job. Not knowing where to find another job, he had decided to take his life so his family could collect his insurance. Just before leaving his home he swallowed a handful of sleeping pills. Hoping to stay awake until he found a cliff by the road, he intended to drive over it and kill himself.

Because of a lost job, that young father lost his dream. But thanks to a minister and his wife who cared, he was able to dream again. He was won to a saving faith in Christ. Later he found new employment to support his family again.

Whatever your age or problem, make a down payment on a dream. Most of the great inventions can be traced back to a dream. We often scold children for daydreaming. But when a person dreams a good dream and makes the dream come true, the world is blessed.

Travel today is fast and convenient because the Wright brothers dreamed they could build a flying machine. Now people can go to almost any place in the world on jet planes.

Henry Ford had the dream of mass producing a car that common people could afford. As a result almost every family in America today owns one or more cars.

A boy sitting under a tree followed a dream that he could make a machine that would help his loved ones hear better. Alexander Graham Bell later made his dream come true by inventing the telephone. Sometimes I enjoy phoning from Texas to California, just to talk for a few minutes with my daughter. Then I think back to pioneer days when young people left the East to come West and find land and new opportunity. Many never saw or heard from their loved ones again.

Our generation witnessed the fulfilled dream of sending men into space. Dreams made science fiction a reality. In our daily lives we enjoy the technology that resulted from these explorations. The future may reveal additional benefits. The capability to dream and make them come true is one way God set man above the other creatures.

Sunday school leaders can inspire us to think big and go out to win people for Christ. Evangelists of our day have big dreams of presenting Christ to multitudes. Over radio and television they share their dreams with the listening world.

Because of their vision people throng to vast crusades. We also need dreams for our local churches and a willingness to work together to make those dreams come true.

God used the dream of a powerful ruler to call the king's attention to Daniel. Because with God's help Daniel could interpret the dream, the king honored him by giving him a high position in the court.

God discerns the thoughts and intents of the heart. It is good to dream and make our dreams come true if we aspire to make the world a better place. Someone wisely said: "The largest room in the world is the room for self-improvement." We can all dream of making the world a better place, and the way to start is with improving ourselves.

A young minister dreamed of being called to a certain church that had no pastor. He wrote letters telling about his education and abilities, but no one in the church seemed interested. He was in despair. But one day as he was praying, God seemed to say, "Go yourself and meet the people."

He and his wife drove fifty miles to this church. They went to the homes of several leaders and told them how much they wanted a church to pastor. The people asked them to come back on the next Sunday. They liked the way the young man preached, so they hired him as their pastor.

An older preacher later chided, "That just isn't the way it is done." But the young pastor responded: "I dreamed of being a pastor, and I worked my way through two schools, so why couldn't I go out and make my dream come true?" This young man was the best pastor that church had ever had.

Dare to make a down payment on a dream. Prepare yourself for the results. Then pray and work hard to make it come true.

Dreams

Dreams while one's sleeping: sometimes they're nightmares;
   Dreams with eyes staring in sad, anxious hope;
Dreams of achievement, or putting on airs;
   Dreams mean so much, as with problems we grope.

Idle daydreams may push into the brain;
   Aimless and pointless, they pilfer the mind;
Whirlwind aircastles are clouds without rain:
   Lazy old dreams, like a check that's unsigned.

Dreams, to be helpful, need purpose and point:
   Blueprinted plans of the work you would do;
Good inspirations need muscle and joint
   If you expect them to really come true.

                                        J. T. Bolding

10
Who Pulls the Wagon?
(Witnessing)

What man of you, having an hundred sheep, if he lose one of them, doth not leave the ninety and nine in the wilderness, and go after that which is lost, until he find it? (Luke 15:4).

Two young children received a red wagon for Christmas. At first, the parents pulled the wagon with both children in it. Then they suggested that their son, since he was older, pull the wagon and let his sister ride.

One day the little girl took the wagon out of the yard alone. She pulled it down the sidewalk for a short way. Growing tired, she got in the wagon and sat down. No one was there to pull the wagon. She started crying. Then she started calling out, "Bobby, come and find me, I'm lost."

Many people out in the world are lost, including young people. As long as they stayed at home, their parents pulled the wagon. They were told what to do, where to go. Money was given to them; a home and food were furnished.

Like the little girl, the day came when they felt sure they could pull the wagon of life alone. Out into the big glittering world they plunged. They found life harder than they had imagined. Some crawled into the wagon and waited, others called for help. Still others attempted to explore life with the wrong companions. Some were loved and helped through the witnessing and caring of Christians.

A young father talked to me about his teenage daughter. He had a good job and could give her anything she wanted (within reason, of course). Although he did indulge her too much, he felt that she should get a summer job and learn to work. His son, two years younger than the daughter, had a part-time job. In other words, he couldn't understand why his daughter didn't learn to pull the wagon.

In our church we have over two thousand people attending Sunday school. The pastor encourages people to come on Monday nights and then go out to contact families and gain new members. Although the leader is pleased when one hundred volunteer to go visiting, the fact remains that the rest of the two thousand just sit in the wagon and let the one hundred do the pulling.

Christians are those "To whom God would make known what is the riches of the glory of this mystery among the Gentiles; which is Christ in you, the hope of glory" (Col. 1:27). To unsaved people, salvation through Christ's blood is a mystery. They may rebuff us when we try to explain the plan of salvation to them. Or, they may ask us never to come back. But they can't keep us from praying for them. Some, with the help of God's Spirit, will respond—to believe and understand the way of salvation.

Too many people around us are getting more and more wrapped up in sin. They do not know about Jesus and how to call on Him. How can some believers say, "I don't know anyone I can witness to"?

The challenge of sharing our Christian faith can be accepted by ordinary people like you and me. We can look around as we go about our daily life. Most of us meet a lot of people in the course of a week. We can and must discover ways to let them know we are servants of God. You can start by inviting them to your church services.

We find what we look for!

> "Oh, are we in our daily life
> Living as we really should,
> Oh, Lord, are we just going about
> Or going about doing good?"

Gifts

Abundantly ours are the gifts of our Lord:
  Forgiveness of sin and the power to live
In peace and contentment which He can accord,
  With joy overflowing He only can give.

His gifts: Oh, what treasures of love He'll provide,
  Of health and ability; freedom of will;
Our privilege given to think and decide,
  With guidance and help to His purpose fulfill.

These gifts really need our responsible care,
  So guard them and use them the way that you
    should;
They're for the world's blessing and so don't you dare
  To squander them just for your own personal
    good.

J. T. Bolding

11
What Doth It Profit?

What doth it profit, my brethren, though a man say he hath faith, and have not works? can faith save him? If a brother or sister be naked, and destitute of daily food, and one of you say unto them, Depart in peace, be ye warmed and filled; notwithstanding ye give them not those things which are needful to the body; what doth it profit? (James 2:14, 15, 16).

Two men were talking about how a college education had failed their children. One had a son who had finished college but was unable to find a job in his chosen career. He worked on his father's farm, but he was trained for a job in business.

The other man had a daughter, who had found a good job after graduation and worked hard. But she had been sent to school to find a husband. At that she had failed.

"So what did it profit us?" one of the fathers asked.

James points out that believing there is a Christ, a heaven, and a hell may not be enough. If we are real followers of Christ, we will also have good works as an expression of our faith. A true Christian heart will not turn needy people away. We are to share with them. James did not ask us to give luxuries to the destitute, but only to meet their basic needs.

We all need kind words at times. But kind words become hollow or cruel without kind deeds to back them up (v. 16).

50

What do kind words profit one who is turned away hungry and weak?

A group of men from Lubbock traveled three hundred and fifty miles to Paris, Texas, after Paris had been devastated by a tornado. Three of the men owned chain saws and took the saws with them. In Paris they cleared away many of the huge old trees that had blown down. In one house lived an old couple. They were trapped inside since they were too feeble to climb over the limbs and trunks of fallen trees near the house. When those men left, however, their yard was cleared and made attractive again. These men could have decided not to go to Paris. They could have rationalized: "What are one or two cleanup jobs more or less in a whole town torn to pieces?" What doth it profit? But their efforts enabled the old couple to get out of their house. The men who worked felt elated because they had helped.

Some people are Monday morning quarterbacks. They go to church on Sunday, but they go away with a critical spirit—telling all who will listen what the minister did wrong, that the music was much too loud, and how some members irritated them. What did it profit the quarterbacks to attend church? There has to be some spiritual response to the worship service or one goes away with an empty heart.

The church one of my granddaughters attends is small; their best attendance may reach one hundred and fifty. Yet the youth put on special musical programs and attend seminars and other wholesome events of interest to them. Although small, this church meets the needs within the membership. What doth it profit churches, or families, if they fail to meet the needs of their members?

Good works is faith in action. Good works is not only praying for others but also providing genuine assistance. During World War II, a young minister left his family and his church, where the people loved him, because he felt it was his patriotic duty to encourage and minister to the boys who were fighting.

After being away overseas for several years, he came home with a discharge. He went to a friend, a minister he had known before the war. This minister had stayed home and had a good church.

He asked his friend to help him get a position with a church. The friend offered to pray for him to find work, but he did not have time to dictate a letter of recommendation. What did it profit that man to be a minister or a friend if he gave no time to help someone with an urgent need.

The former chaplain contacted another friend who also was a pastor. This friend made a trip to a pastorless church and told them about the chaplain who had returned home. The church soon called the young man to be their pastor. One man felt too self-important to help his friend; the other went the second mile to provide genuine assistance. Never tell someone in need that you will pray for them if you are not willing to help them. The Lord calls us to minister for Him. He challenges us to back up our faith with action.

12
Hold Up His Hands

And it came to pass, when Moses held up his hand, that Israel prevailed: and when he let down his hand, Amalek prevailed. But Moses hands were heavy, and they took a stone, and put it under him, and he sat thereon; And Aaron and Hur stayed up his hands . . . until the going down of the sun   (Exod. 17:11, 12).

The Amalekites came to fight the Israelites. Moses was the leader of the Israelites and Joshua was head of the fighting men. Moses told Joshua to choose some of the men for battle with the enemy. Moses promised to stand on top of a hill and hold in his hand the staff of the Lord.

As long as Moses held up his hands, the battle went in favor of the Israelites. But Moses became weary and could no longer stand with his hands raised. Then Aaron and Hur gave Moses a stone to sit on while on each side of him they held up his hands until finally the victory was won by Joshua. What if Aaron and Hur had not held up the hands of Moses? The battle would have been lost.

We have opportunities almost every day to hold up the hands of some one who needs our support or assistance. Although we're not involved with guns or swords, someone may need our help in the battle of life.

A few years ago I was in the hospital for the removal of two malignant tumors. As the doctor was making arrangements for the surgery, he said: "We will need a special nurse for the nights."

"She already has a special nurse for the nights," my husband told him. "Put a cot in this room. She will receive quality care."

My husband slept in my room every night and was the best nurse in the world. He held my hand, literally and figuratively, during those ten days of trouble. Because he was there, I felt safe and secure. Hadn't he cared for me over forty years? He would keep on.

It is natural to hold up the hands of family members when they are in trouble. We also need to look for those outside our family who need our help. The world about us is filled with people who, like Moses, have carried a heavy load a long time and will fall down from exhaustion unless someone helps to hold up their hands.

A school girl was walking home slowly after school. Each step seemed a burden. Then a girlfriend came running behind her, grabbed her hand, and said: "Let's run." The girl seemed to come to life as she ran with her friend holding her hand. Do you know of someone who needs your cheer and encouragement right now?

An enlisted man named Lovell from Oklahoma says he will never forget his army sergeant. During a summer training jump at Fort Campbell, Kentucky, the paratrooper sergeant saw that Lovell's parachute had collapsed. The sergeant grabbed him. Both soldiers dropped several hundred feet to safety under the sergeant's parachute. Helping hands saved a life that day.

People in all walks of life need helping hands to make the difference. Near Amarillo is a place called Cal Farley's Boys' Ranch. Mr. and Mrs. Farley have died, but the wonderful home they founded for boys who had no place to go still operates. The Farleys held out loving hands to boys who were lonely

and hungry. Their hands fed them, assured them, and taught
them how to work and study.

My Influence

My life shall touch a dozen lives
    Before this day is done;
Leave countless marks for good or ill
    Ere sets the evening sun.

So this the wish I always wish,
    The prayer I ever pray;
Lord, may my life help other lives
    It touches by the way.

Unknown

In many ways we can hold up the hands of those about us.
We can hold up the hands of our church leaders by expressing
gratitude and encouragement for their service. Other people
may need us just to listen. A family encountering illness or
grief might appreciate food brought into them. You may think
of other ways to be helpful.

It was little I had but I gave from my store
To those who had less, or who needed it more;
And I came through Death laughing, and beyond the grave
In riches unmeasured I found more than I gave!

Unknown

13
Walk in High Places

The Lord God is my strength, and he will make my feet like hinds' feet, and he will make me to walk upon mine high places (Hab. 3:19).

This verse is translated in a modern version as "he will . . . bring me safely over the mountain" (*The Living Bible*).

When I was a child we often went to our city park for picnics or just to play. Then our community was a safer place. Widespread crime, caused by greed and drugs, had not invaded it. In the park a foot bridge crossed a small creek. When I was first old enough to walk, I used the bridge and felt a strong sense of accomplishment. (I enjoyed that bridge even more after I was grown, when I had a sweetheart to walk with me.)

In recent years, here in Lubbock, I took my grandchildren to a nearby park. To my surprise, we discovered a playground climber, which reached about twenty feet into the air. My grandchildren enjoyed playing on that the most. They soon reached the top, looked out over the park, and called out: "Look, Grannie, how high I am!"

Our human nature prompts us to climb a mountain or to take an elevator to the top of a tall building for a commanding view of the surroundings. But I want us to think of the high places in life we long to walk over.

After childhood and youth have passed, we come, figuratively speaking, to high places of life, sometimes after walking through the valley. Most young married couples think of the high places they want to walk on, such as owning a home, having children, or traveling abroad.

Or, for example, I know a young man who is walking the highest road in my opinion. After graduating from college, he left a good job to go to Africa as a missionary to win the lost. He is having success. He trains young African men to preach effectively. Yet, as I think of him walking in high places, he nonetheless makes a great sacrifice in personal comforts and even health. I remember others who help this missionary. A young woman collects money to keep him in Africa. Many other friends give money to support his work. They also are walking in high places as they serve in their own way.

And, I recall Chung Feng Wang, a boy living in Formosa. He was a child with a great mountain to climb. He was born with a cleft lip and palate and was unable to hear, speak, or smile. Other children made fun of him and refused to play with him.

But Mr. Bardfield, also a deaf mute, visited Formosa. He saw Chung and felt sorry for him. He took a picture of Chung, and after returning to his job in the United States he started raising money for medical help. Dr. Vincent Pennisi, a noted plastic surgeon, agreed to perform the series of operations. A deaf-mute family promised to keep Chung in their home while he was in the states. U.S. Army wives on Formosa worked to raise money to send Chung to America. The high road he had to travel—just to be able to smile—was very long. But God sent just the right people to walk over that mountain with him.

When you got out of bed this morning you might have felt you could not face the day. But remember, God is there to walk with you if you let Him. Or, you might have the opportunity to walk with someone who needs you.

One morning, a five-year-old handicapped child wandered away from her home. As soon as the mother discovered her missing from the sand box, she started looking. She searched frantically, walking and running until she was exhausted. After thirty minutes she called the police.

Meanwhile, two women, talking in their front yards, saw the little girl walking in the street. They ran to her and brought her to safety. Since she could not talk well enough to tell her name, the women called the police. Soon the child was safely back with her mother. The mother wrote a nice letter, which was published in the local paper, thanking the women for rescuing her child off the street.

There are, however, other phases of walking in high places beside helping people over the mountains of life's problems. One, for example, is parenting.

If you train your children to think of accomplishing good and useful things, they likely will walk in higher places. They will study harder and be either leaders or good followers. "Train up a child in the way he should go, and when he is old he will not depart from it" (Prov. 23:7).

Another way of walking the high places is through service and unselfishness. As a pastor's wife for more than fifty years, I have known both wealthy people and poor people. One wealthy lady, a model of selfishness, called me almost daily for fifteen years. I often left the typewriter to listen to her complaints. Her husband was a bedfast man, and although she hired a nurse for him, she would get lonely. Not once in those years, however, did she show any real interest in me or my family. She just talked about herself.

Another lady I know, not rich or even well off, takes time to visit nursing homes and plays the piano for the patients. She enjoys her visits with the bedridden. The rich lady, by contrast, although she also could play the piano and could, at least, afford to buy cookies for the old folks, would only say when I suggested she visit this nursing home, "Let their children take care of them."

We do not all have the same talents, but we can all find some way to make the world a better place.

High Places

Some folk are like tight rope walkers,
    High o'erhead in circus tent;
Others spend their lives as talkers
    As if they were heaven sent.

Some folk are like mountain climbers
    Searching for a peak that's new;
Others are like good pump primers,
    Pushing us our best to do.

Some folks climb to heights of power,
    Leaders in the things they do;
Some stand ready for each hour
    Challenged by the larger view.

God walks with us through hard places,
    He gives us grace for each new day,
Helping us to run our races,
    And be faithful all the way.

God walks with us o'er the mountains;
  Guides, upholds us through the vales;
Helping us to find his fountains,
  Blessing us through rugged gales.

J. T. Bolding

14

The Three P's—
Propagation!
Preparation!
Preservation!

And God blessed them, saying, Be fruitful, and multiply, and fill the waters in the seas, and let fowl multiply in the earth (Gen. 1:22).

Study to show thyself approved unto God, a workman that needeth not to be ashamed, rightly dividing the word of truth (II Tim. 2:15).

The Lord will preserve him, and keep him alive; and he shall be blessed upon the earth: and thou will not deliver him unto the will of his enemies (Ps. 41:2).

For the family, for the world, and for the future, we need the three P's: propagation, preparation, and preservation.

Propagation. God gave man the order to multiply and replenish the earth. He did not want His great big beautiful world to sit vacant and idle. He wanted it filled with people, animals, birds, and fish.

A few years ago, statistics told us that the last child in a family is born, on the average, when the mother is twenty-six years old. The average age for a child to leave home is seventeen. The average couple lives with an empty nest for over thirty years.

So, what are we to do when our children are raised and family obligations are not so heavy? Many women go to work and start new careers. Many couples start traveling and living for fun and relaxation. We could, however, start thinking about another kind of propagation—to help spread the gospel. Jesus suggested something we might do to receive great blessings. He said: "Go ye into all the world, and preach the gospel to every creature" (Mark 16:15). We are not to settle down in a pew on Sunday and then forget our church and Lord the rest of the week. We are to help the Christian world multiply.

I recall that a number of years ago our church had two services each Sunday morning. The early service was very popular with nurses, waitresses, and others who had to work on Sundays. They could come early to worship and then go on to work.

But a new pastor came, who did not want to preach twice on Sunday mornings. He cancelled the early service. After that, many people had no chance to attend services. Our church let one good opportunity to spread the gospel go.

Preparation. Almost everything works out better if we prepare for it. Often it's hard to explain to teenagers why they need to stay in school and prepare for life. When young adults go out into life without completing their education, they have two strikes against them before the game has really started.

Preparation for our church life is very important. One time, when my husband and I were younger, we were asked to go to a small church and conduct a Bible school for children. For days we worked to get all our plans made and our material ready to go.

When we arrived at the church, however, we found that the pastor had been busy trying to get another position and had forgotten to announce the Bible school. So we asked some of the members to help us, and we spent all Sunday afternoon going from house to house inviting the children to come the next morning. God blessed our efforts, and we had a successful Bible school with many children led to trust Christ as their Savior.

Another small church I know required all the workers to get together well before it was time for the Bible school to start. They had every day planned—down to the last song and game. They were, at least, not so tired out by last-minute, frantic efforts. They had prepared.

My hairdresser told me she had not seen her father in four years. I encouraged her to make the effort and go. She dreaded going because her father had married again after her mother died, and her stepmother did not make her feel welcome. At last she and her sister and her sister's four-year-old daughter decided to go.

She called her father and asked him if they could come. "I'll let you talk to my wife," he said, and handed the phone to her.

"You probably won't like a thing I fix, but come on," she invited hesistantly.

So the two women, who worked every day just to have shelter and food, went to see their father. My friend told me later that she had a very good time. Her stepmother had made a plan for each meal. She had cooked all day before the girls arrived. She had food ready in the freezer. As a result she felt confident of her ability to serve good meals, and relaxed. It is wise to prepare for any project or situation in life.

Preservation. The psalmist David said, "The Lord will protect him and preserve his life; he will bless him in the land

and not surrender him to the desire of his foes" (Psalm 41:2, NIV).

David complained about his enemies' treachery. He had gone to the king's palace as a young boy to play sweet music and be a friend. But the king had turned against him, and David had to flee for his life and hide out in the wilderness. Yet, he wrote of his conviction that God will preserve him.

When we read our daily papers, we often feel frightened and wonder what is going to become of our world. Ten or fifteen years ago, alone and without fear, I drove across town or even, a few times, to other towns after dark. Today crime is so prevalent that we lock our car doors when we are driving home after church. Yet, if we read the Scriptures, we know God is going to preserve His own.

One night in December of 1980, our bedroom door opened and a strange man stood silhouetted against the light. I was awake and started screaming. My husband woke up and almost had a heart attack trying to find something with which to protect ourselves.

The intruder was not inclined to fight, and ran out of the house. We felt relieved. But he had been all through our house and turned on all the lights until he came to the closed bedroom door. The intruder had pried open a glass door and a wooden door without making enough noise for us to hear.

God preserved us that night; we easily could have been harmed. It's good to know that our times are in God's hands.

15
Problems and Challenges

Also they have shut up the doors of the porch, and put out the lamps, and have not burned incense nor offered burnt offerings in the holy place unto the God of Israel   (II Chron. 29:7).

King Hezekiah began his reign over Judah when he was twenty-five years old. The Bible tells us "He trusted in the Lord God of Israel; so that after him was none like him among all the kings of Judah, nor any that were before him" (II Kings 18:5).

When Hezekiah came to the throne, he immediately looked about to see how he could improve his kingdom. We are used to that. Politicians tell us, before they are elected, what needs to be done. After election day, some of those elected officials suddenly can't see what needs improving.

But King Hezekiah was a man of action. He considered problems to be challenges. The first problem was a neglected temple. The young king looked at the house of worship and said in effect, "You have put out the lights."

The king was angry. Where people should have been worshiping God, the doors were shut and the lights turned off.

One of his first acts, after he saw the condition of the temple, was to clean it and repair it. Then Hezekiah called all the people to the temple site, to offer sacrifices and worship God.

The lights were shining again in the temple. The people would again be blessed by God. Hezekiah had to do one more thing to show his faith in God. He destroyed the brazen serpent (said to be the one Moses had put up in the wilderness for the people to look at and be healed). It had become a symbol of adoration in place of God.

In some churches today many lights are out. Worldly pleasures have put them out. Some churches have failed to preach and teach biblical truth. Some people who attend church on Sunday morning have never attended an evening service. They have never driven up the street after dark to see the lights shining through the beautiful windows. Many Americans come to church only on Easter and Christmas. They are missing the blessing of meeting God each Sunday in the house of worship.

A modern-day Hezekiah is the minister who was called to a new church. He noticed very few were attending services. Instead of going out and saying ugly things about the people, he started visiting them. They had never known what it was to have a pastor visit in their homes.

He took an interest in their problems and in their joys. After he had visited every home, he noticed a few new faces in the services each Sunday. Then he sent out letters asking the men to help clean up around the church building and asking the women to clean the inside. Enough workers came that people passing by noticed how clean and nice things looked.

One Sunday he appointed some committees to plan a homecoming. Church members worked enthusiastically for that event and invited many people. Old friends came from many miles away. Food was plentiful, and good speakers were enjoyed.

All the while, people were being drawn close to the Lord. The young man never let the lights go out, and a church, which had been dying, grew and flourished.

In all walks of life, if we determine that our problems can be challenges, we will win the battle. Many people are too easily defeated by a problem. For example, my friend Joyce went to a neighbor's house across the street and asked the father to keep his son at home. While she was away at work the child had come over and rubbed mud on her newly painted house.

"You will have to call the police," the man told her, "I can't do anything with him, but he is afraid of the police."

"Are you saying that you can't make a four-year-old child obey you?"

The man saw his child only as a problem; he felt no challenge to train him to be a good child.

Each new day will have its problems; yet we can choose to enjoy the challenges. Heartsill Wilson gives us this insight:

This is the beginning of a new day. God has given me this day to use as I will. I can waste it or use it for good. What I do today is important because I'm exchanging a day of my life for it.

Some people live in yesterday land, others live for tomorrow, but many forget how important today is. Let today be a challenge to live it to the fullest. Keep the lights of excitement and goodwill burning brightly.

16

Tomorrow: A New Experience

... For unto whomsoever much is given, of him shall be much required ... (Luke 12:48).

Then Peter said, "Silver and gold have I none; but such as I have give I thee; ... " (Acts 3:6).

Give and it shall be given unto you; good measure, pressed down, and shaken together, and running over, shall men give into your bosom (Luke 6:39).

W hen I phoned a friend in the country to thank her for a favor, her daughter answered. I thanked her and asked her to tell her mother when she came in.

"Mrs. Bolding, Daddy is out planting the garden today, and he has your name on one row," the daughter told me.

I felt good all day knowing my name was on one row in Tom's garden. Through the years he has brought us many nice fruits and vegetables from his small farm.

Life is sweeter when we know someone cares about our well being. What could I do for my friends? I can pray for them. I can give them books and magazines. I can let them know how very much I appreciate their kindness. Each day the body hungers and thirsts; each day it is fed. But the soul has a hunger of its own.

Recently, on a newscast, we heard about a baby being born so badly deformed that the parents and doctor decided not to feed it. The baby soon died.

I do not know the details, and I have no right to pass judgment on the parents. It was sad for them to dream and hope through nine months for a healthy, normal baby, and then feel the bitter disappointment of a severely deformed infant.

Some parents, however, have strong healthy children physically, but they have never been fed spiritual food. A good cook would not think of feeding her family the same food every day. She will vary the menu and try new dishes, or new ways to prepare food. So with soul food. We must plan and be alert for new spiritual experiences. Start today!

God knows people need new experiences and changes. God designed variety for the earth. Spring changes to summer, summer to autumn, and autumn to winter. Each season has its own wonderful traits for us to enjoy. Nature's diversity helps make us ready for each change and each new experience.

Therefore don't feed your soul on the same familiar Scripture. Read a variety of Bible passages. Read about the exciting events of God preparing a people for His own, and about God sending a Redeemer to a lost world. Could any TV show or novel be more exciting? Don't pray the same prayer over and over. Develop and grow in your prayer life.

I recently heard the expression "Be a go-giver, not a go-getter." Wouldn't it be a new experience if each of us resolved to give something away each day. This would include not just material gifts, but gifts of cheer and emotional support as well.

"I have barely enough for myself, how can I give something away each day," you might say.

What did Peter say? "Such as I have give I thee."

Only a Smile

It was only a smile that he gave me,
    But to me it was wondrous indeed:
It restored ebbing hopes e'er so quickly,
    And fulfilled my heart's crying need.

Selected

Do you feel that you are completely out of smiles? How sad if you have no more words of encouragement to share.

Yesterday I heard of a little girl who went to visit a friend who had lost her father. She handed her friend a small home-made card with crayon pictures of flowers she had drawn on it. At the bottom she had printed a verse she learned in Sunday school: "He careth for you."

The card cost no money, only time. Like this girl, if you look each day for a new experience—a chance to help some-one—you will find many opportunities, and you will be hap-pier.

Do you know someone who sparkles? They laugh and make those around them happy. Would you like to be a sparkler? Start by being a "go-giver."

Why were there fewer divorces fifty or one-hundred years ago? It's partially because men and women were so busy and trying to meet the needs of their families that they had little time for discontent. They were "go-givers." They had no pen-sions. When a neighbor became ill, neighbors took turns nurs-ing the one in need.

Think for a moment. When you were young what dreams did you have of a new experience for tomorrow? Did you dream of a lifetime companion, owning a home, travel, or being a leader?

I remember a king mentioned in the Bible. He was a good king. David dreamed about making his nation strong and about building a beautiful temple for his people.

One day, when he was idle, the devil turned his head from his dream. He saw a beautiful woman. In his desire to possess her, he forgot his plans and dreams. He forgot he was supposed to be a "go-giver" for the people he ruled.

The Bible describes how Jesus went forth among the people. He was moved with compassion toward them, and he healed their sick. As Jesus' disciple you are needed somewhere, by someone. Keep on the alert for those who need your help.

Consolation

If none were sick and none were sad
    What service could we render?
I think if we were always glad
    We scarcely could be tender.
Did our beloved never need
    Our patient ministration
Earth would grow cold, and miss indeed
    Its sweetest consolation.
If sorrow never claimed our heart,
    And every wish were granted,
Patience would die and hope depart
    Life would be disenchanted.

Unknown

17
The Storm, The Calm

A furious squall came up, and the waves broke over the boat, so that it was nearly swamped. Jesus was in the stern, sleeping on a cushion. The disciples woke him and said to him, "Teacher don't you care if we drown!"

He got up, rebuked the wind and said to the waves, "Quiet! be still!" Then the wind died down and it was completely calm
(Mark 4:37-39, NIV).

Jesus had taught all day long at the seashore. The crowd was so large that Jesus got into a boat and sat in it while He taught, a small distance away from His listeners along the shore. At the end of the day, tired and worn. He asked His disciples to take Him to the other side of the lake. They started out across the lake, with other little boats following along. A squall attacked suddenly. Waves began breaking into their boat. They were in danger of losing their lives. Jesus, tired and weary, was fast sleep, resting from His day's work and appearing confident that all was well.

But His followers, terrified, could stand it no longer. They woke Jesus and asked, "Teacher, don't you care if we drown?"

How many times in your life have you faced hardship and there seemed to be no way out? Do you remember praying something like, "Dear God please help me. Don't you care?" It's like the first stanza of this hymn:

> Does Jesus care when your heart is pained
> Too deeply for mirth or song
> As the burdens press,
> And the cares distress,
> And the way grows weary and long?

But the second stanza reassures us.

> O yes, He cares, I know He cares,
> His heart is touched by my grief;
> When the days are weary,
> The long night dreary,
> I know my Saviour cares.

Frank E. Graeff and
J. Lincoln Hall, 1928

Jesus did care for His disciples. He spoke immediately to the storm and commanded the waves to be still. Then all was calm.

Storms come into our lives today and we need faith in Jesus to see us through. For example, a friend of mine went on a short vacation trip. Since her car is old, I feared that it would have mechanical problems. After she returned my first question was: "Did the car work all right?"

"No," she answered. "I had trouble six miles from a station. But I turned my problem over to the Lord. I told him it was unsafe for me to be stranded in the middle of nowhere, alone. Then I started the car and drove on into town. The car was smoking. There I found a mechanic to fix it well enough for me to get home."

Then she shared a sad story. She was adopted as a small baby and her adopted mother died about the time she finished high school. But the father didn't care about her, so she was out on her own. Yet she affirms, "I have passed through many a storm, but I love God. He has been my refuge and strength."

Here's another example. One of my husband's minister friends has a large family of grown children. A few years back, this minister lost his church. All five of those grown children started working to find another church for their daddy. They asked for help from all their preacher friends. I am sure all were praying for the Lord's help. Soon their prayers were answered, and their lives were calm again.

Some of the great achievements of life were made by people who passed through storms of disappointment, trouble, and loss. They maintained a hope for success and they persevered through it all. We will succeed if we take the difficulties we encounter in stride, continue to work toward our goals, and wait for the calm.

We should not create unnecessary storms in our lives by trying to be better or more successful than others. We can focus our efforts on trying to improve ourselves. Each of us has a different level of ability and we can remain calm in the knowledge that we are living up to our own best.

When the storm on the Sea of Galilee threatened death and destruction, the disciples knew whom to ask for help. But like we do so often, they waited a while before they asked. How much time would we save if we would live so close to the Lord that requesting His help would always be our first thought.

My mother taught me that lesson well. One of the most calming things I remember about my childhood was hearing my mother sing. She never had a maid to help her. She sang as she washed our clothes with a rub board and tub. She sang as she churned butter or as she shelled beans. I believed every song she sang, and they gave me strength as I was growing up. Long before I was old enough to give my heart to Jesus, I believed God would take care of me. Why? Because my mother would frequently sing the hymn that begins this way: "Be not dismayed what e'er be tide, God will take care of you." Be careful about the songs you sing and the words you say in the presence of your children. The impression on them is lasting. In their times of storm, the right words you may have said or sung will bring calm into their lives.

When we are faced with a storm we need to have good shipmates. The men in the boat with Christ were His follow-ers. They had left their families to be with Jesus. They were good shipmates. The Bible narrative states that they took him in the boat, even as he was (tired from the long day). But didn't He make a wonderful shipmate in time of the storm. Choose your shipmates well, and be sure not to forget the Savior.

Storms

Storms and rough weather may come where we are;
   Sorrows may cast dark shadows now and then.
Heartaches and illness may not stay afar,
   Life may be difficult time and again.

Ah, but the memories of God's tender love,
   Which has surrounded on other bad days.
It builds up courage with help from above
   And the bright sunlight across our path plays.

So let's remember God's help in the past,
   Never forgetting His love and His care;
Trusting His providence, knowing at last
   We can depend upon Him if we dare.

J. T. Bolding

18
House Cleaning—Today

Create in me a clean heart, O God; and renew a right spirit within me. Cast me not away from thy presence; and take not thy holy spirit from me. Restore unto me the joy of thy salvation; and uphold me with thy free spirit (Ps. 51:10-12).

Susan keeps her house extraordinarily clean. Her guests wonder whether it is permissible to sit on a chair or walk on her sparkling linoleum. But her heart is another matter. Usually her attitude is cluttered with grudges and resentments.

Let's think about heart-cleaning. We need to ask God, as the psalmist did: "Create in me a clean heart." What does a clean heart demand of us? It demands that we throw away and forget envy, greed, jealousy, and anger.

A recently retired friend said: "We want our life to be simple now." So she cleaned her closets, and her husband cleaned the garage. Then they had a huge garage sale. They didn't want so many things to clean over, under, and around.

If we would stand away and take a good look at our hearts, how many things would we put out in the trash and forget forever? If we washed the windows of our heart we would see, in a different light, the things we harbor and gripe about. Or, if we could just see another person's side of the picture, we might become kinder and more understanding.

Only Today

Yesterday's sun went down last night
And the sun of tomorrow is yet to rise:
Only the sky of today is bright
Over the path where our journey lies.

We who would come to the goal at last
Must wait not to dream beside the way:
There is hope in the future and help from the past.
But for work there is only today.

Unknown

If we desire our hearts to be cleansed and pure, the bad habits we have accumulated must be ejected. By contrast some people hang on to negative habits, such as criticising their friends behind their backs. What an ugly thing to do! If you are like me, you want your friends to be true to you while you are absent. A real friend consistently has something constructive to say.

Another poor habit some people have is bearing false witness. They disclaim telling an outright lie, but they imply bad things about others. A person with a cleansed heart will pray and put forth the effort to break such bad habits. Before you speak or act, think to yourself: Would I want others to treat me that way? Would Jesus be pleased with my words and actions?

After bad habits are overcome, a person with a clean heart welcomes and develops good habits. What comes next? Better health! People with clean hearts and good habits usually are healthier. They will relate to the world with good humor and find their lives happier as a result.

Have you visited a home where the family seems glad to be together? They seem eager to help each other in projects and problems. In homes where hearts are clean, bad habits are frowned on, people are healthier, and there is more happiness.

"There are two kinds of guests—those who bring happiness *wherever* they go and those who bring happiness *whenever* they go." Our world desperately needs more people willing to work to have clean hearts, good habits, healthy bodies, and happy homes.

Being a Christian will help you to be a better, happier person. You will belong to the greatest movement in the world. You can be as happy as you make up your mind to be. As an immersed tea bag transforms the water, let your cleansed heart transform those around you.

Spring Cleaning

When springtime comes, the cleaning bug
  Bites housewives here and there;
They wash the windows, beat the rug;
  The place gets special care.

When Christ comes into sinful hearts,
  The cleaning will begin.
For when he saves, folk make new starts:
  New life is ushered in.

The difference that the Lord will make
  When he has entered in,
Becomes apparent and we take
  A turn away from sin.

Now when this new life is begun,
  His grace fulfills our dreams;
Our sins forgiven through God's dear son,
  As He our soul redeems.

J. T. Bolding

19
What Is Your Life?
(Graduation)

Whereas ye know not what shall be on the morrow. For what is your life? It is even a vapour that appeareth for a little time, and then vanisheth away   (James 4:14).

And all thy children shall be taught of the Lord; and great shall be the peace of thy children   (Isa. 54:13).

If someone wrote and published a book about your past twelve years of school life, would you be willing to have it placed in the bookstores for others to read? Do you remember the way you behaved on your first day at school? Would you be embarrassed to have others read your life story? Would your story be sad, or happy, or unflattering?

Today you close the book on your elementary and high school days. You are going to enter an even harder school. You will have to meet and compete with different types of people. In the Scripture above, James asks all of us this question: What is your life?

What is your purpose? What is your program? What is the goal you wish to fulfill?

Two of my granddaughters recently graduated from high school. Both girls have dreams. One especially enjoys studying and plans to take a demanding college course that will prepare her to be a chemical engineer. The other granddaughter chose to study nursing. She thoroughly enjoys people. She likes to talk and to hear others talk. Each girl made her choice of a career. Each made a wise decision.

What is your life? Largely what you make it to be. Think about the things for which you are gifted. What are your stronger talents? Pick a worthy purpose for your life. Be sure it is one that will make a better world, help others, and fulfill your own dreams and hopes. When you have selected your purpose, hang on to it. You might, however, change your career plans a year or two from now. That's okay. Many college students change majors after the first or second year in school.

After you have decided on a career, plan your course to achieve your objective. Follow a program that will include proper study hours. Allow time for some physical exercise and also time for making new friends.

After you have selected a worthy purpose and decided on a plan to accomplish that purpose, you also will have a prize to struggle for. Crown your days with victory and honor. To gain victory and honor, you must have a personal commitment to God. That is essential for your strength and salvation. When something you wanted very much fails to come your way, remember the center of your life. God will be there to give you peace and strength. Be a person of faith and courage. Trust in God, for He is your strength.

Our Graduate's Prayer

So many roads where I may go,
   Far more than two or three;
There's one thing now I'd like to know
   Which is the road for me?

There's much to ask; there's much to know,
    Far more than I can see.
To find, should I say "yes" or "no"
    to take the road for me?
I must move on; I cannot stay;
    I pause on bended knee.
"Help me, dear Lord, so I can say,
    This is the road for me."

Author unknown

Looking ahead, you will have new lessons to learn, new problems to face, and new friends to meet. Some friends you will become wary of. Other friends you will cherish and keep for lifetime.

Here are some rules that are helpful for daily life.

The first rule is: *Start the day with prayer.* I hope you have followed this rule through high school. Pray on the bus, in your car, or wherever you find the day starting for you. A moment of prayer will help you think more clearly all day. It will help you remember that your life is sustained by a higher power. The presence and wisdom of that divine power will stay with you all day.

Second rule is: *Try to share a word of praise daily.* As you meet someone during the day—supervisor, working companion, or friend—say a word of praise. Criticism will be heard loudly and often; see that your praise is louder. Praise brings out the best in others. For example, a retarded, young girl wanted to sit at the study table as her brother and sister were preparing their lessons for the next day. One day her brother bought a tablet for her to use. Her sister donated a pencil. Each night the three worked together at the table.

After a few weeks, the two school children discovered that their retarded sister was drawing pictures. She demonstrated that she had a special gift for drawing simple things.

"Look, mother, how well Annie can draw!" they called out. Praising her work, even when she did not do so well, not only brought smiles to her face, but brought out her genuine talent as well.

Here are other rules:

Be friendly. Never fail to show friendliness to others. Some people may be new in town, and lonely.

Be a helper when you're needed. Stay alert to give assistance. But remember to do this wisely. Don't jump into action every time someone asks you to do something. Sometimes it's necessary to say no. Don't be a doormat, to be mistreated and walked on. But when there is a genuine need and you are in a position to help, give of yourself. Look to Jesus as an example of service to others.

Look your best. Most of us enjoy being with nice-looking people. You may not have a closet full of expensive clothes to start out your new life of work or college. But you can look pleasant, clean and neat.

Graduation!

The grand day at last has come.
   Graduation now is near.
Join us as we beat the drum and
   Celebrate this victory dear.

Joyous milestone, so long yearned for.
   Unattainable it seemed.
Day the midnight oil was burned for,
   Like a lighthouse it has gleamed.

Ready now new worlds to conquer.
Set to go for all the best.
Give me grace, dear heavenly Father,
Help me not to fail life's test.

J. T. Bolding

20

Triumphs of the Empty Tomb!

And they found the stone rolled away from the sepulchre. And they entered in, and found not the body of the Lord Jesus (Luke 24:2, 3).

He is not here, but is risen (Luke 24:6).

Thanks be to God, which giveth us the victory through our Lord Jesus Christ (I Cor. 15:57).

We live only a few miles from a large stadium. During the football season, parked cars line the roads and fill the vacant lots and other available space within walking distance of the stadium. One filling-station operator told us that he closes his station on game days and makes more money by charging for parking spaces. Americans love sports and want their favorite team to win.

What a huge crowd would have been gathered at the tomb before that first Easter morning if people had known that the greatest victory ever gained would occur within the next few hours. But, as in our lives, some of our greatest victories are won during the quiet times when only ourselves and the Lord are present.

At the very core of the Jewish religion was their hope for the Messiah to come and restore the kingdom to Israel. The disciples had believed that Jesus was the Messiah. They wanted to be a part of His kingdom. But when they saw His body hanging on the cross, they lost all hope. When Jesus' body was sealed in a tomb, in despair they went away. Their dreams evaporated and they felt that their Master and His cause were totally defeated.

Calvary, however, was not the end of everything for them. Rather, it was a beginning of a great new era. Our God is a God of victory. We know this from our personal experiences. For example, some time ago, a man gave a testimony at our midweek prayer service. He was over fifty years old and he had just lost his job. With children in college and a wife and home to maintain, he needed work and felt only God could find another job for a man of his age. He had gone to the men's prayer breakfast and asked them to concentrate on his need in prayer. He also searched hard to find a new position. After a few weeks, God gave him the victory. He commented: "My new job is much better than my old one. I have better pay and better working conditions. God gave me the victory."

Our victorious Saviour has the ultimate power over death. Does death end all? No. For the Christian death is a new and glorious beginning in a new and perfect place.

On that Easter morning, the sad-hearted women came first to visit the tomb. They were coming to apply spices on the body of Jesus. To their surprise, they found the stone rolled away and the tomb empty. What a victory! Their sorrow turned to joy. Gladness took the place of grief. As the sunrise broke the darkness of night, it symbolized the dawning of a new age. *"Thanks be unto God who giveth us the victory."*

After a ball game some youngsters cry "We won! We won!" as they run to meet their parents. When Mary Magdalene discovered the stone rolled away from the tomb she ran to find Peter and John to tell them the good news. To paraphrase her joyous message she exclaimed, "We won! He is alive!"

Before Christ's stunning victory over death, His followers had turned away feeling defeated because they lost hope. We, too, lose hope when we forget that God is all powerful over death and the events of our lives. We should be alert to the evidence of God's grace in our lives each day. If we do not see miracles happening in our lives today, it is because we are too dull to open our eyes and look about for them.

We started out one April morning driving to our son's house six hundred miles away. Just after we crossed Red river from Texas into Oklahoma we saw clouds of dust in the distance and could tell that the wind was picking up.

When we stopped for gas in Oklahoma City, my husband almost blew over when he opened the car door and tried to get out. The wind velocity was over sixty miles per hour. At last he managed to fill the gas tank and we continued our trip. When we turned off the interstate on a highway going north, the wind did not seem as bad. We kept going.

We believe that God worked a miracle for us that day. On the evening news we heard that a storm had hit Paris, Texas, and ten people were killed. We had traveled very close to Paris. Then we learned that a car on a highway north of us had been blown off the road and both occupants were killed. We continue to thank God for His tender care over His children.

As we experience God's care and grace, let's share these experiences. When the disciples saw Christ after His resurrection and talked to Him, they caught the fire to carry out Christ's commission and do God's work throughout the Roman Empire. Through the centuries the flame continued to spread. Today, the far-reaching influence of Christianity encompasses the whole world. *Hallelujah! What a Savior!*

21
Mother's Day

Forsake not the law of thy mother (Prov. 6:20).

Honor thy father and thy mother; that thy days may be long upon the land which the Lord thy God giveth thee (Exod. 20:12).

Take this child and nurse it for me and I will give thee thy wages" (Exod. 2:9).

My husband and I raised our three children with love, care, and discipline. It warms my heart that today our grown children honor us by loving and respecting us. For example, our son teaches in a large university. He has several degrees to his credit. But to me the fact that he honors his parents is one of the best aspects of his character. When we visit his home, he makes us feel like honored guests. He is kind, patient, and sweet with us even though we are old and have some old-fashioned ideas.

I am proud to have such a son. What can I still do for him? Three times a day, when my husband and I sit at the table to eat, we ask God's special blessings on our three children. What greater gift can we give them now than to ask for God's love and care.

Children first learn what love is and how to love from their mothers and fathers. A godly mother's love remains special and unique in a child's life. No human love is so much like

God's love as the love of a mother for her child. When my mother was a small child, she traveled in a covered wagon with her family to make the run for land in Oklahoma. They arrived a day late, but still were able to buy land at a cheap price. My mother walked over two miles to school every day of her school life. Her years of schooling took her through the eleventh-grade level.

I admired my mother even more after I was grown. I realized how much she had worked to help support her five children through college. The Bible says, "Remember the law of thy mother" (Prov. 1:8). In our household *mother* was a magic word. We respected her wisdom and authority.

Some thoughtless young person might ask, "What do I owe my mother?"

Well, who brought that baby into the world through the pain of childbirth? Who saw to it that food was on the table when that child was hungry? Who followed that child to the door on school day mornings to see that he or she was wearing a warm jacket? "Can a woman forget her child? . . . Yet will I not forget thee" (Isa. 49:15).

Many children have succeeded in life because their mothers had confidence in them. A mother's confidence inspires a child to work harder to succeed. The successful painter Benjamin West said: "My mother's kiss of approval made me a painter."

I guess most mothers are ambitious for their children. In the Bible we have the story of a mother who was too eager for her sons to have the best. The Gospel of Matthew records the story of the mother of James and John. She went to Jesus and asked if her sons could have the highest seats of honor when Jesus established His Kingdom. The mother of James and John was not a bad person, although misguided, and she loved her sons.

We see similar maternal attitudes today. Some mothers support their children through sports, social clubs, or private lessons to help insure their success. Another mother might try subtle bribery by frequently giving gifts to the teacher, hoping that her child will get a bit more attention or, perhaps, better grades.

Other mothers may love their children just as much but they don't have the time to support their children in extracurricular activities. Maybe they have to work every day to keep bread on the table.

My husband and I sense this as we observe children walking to our neighborhood school. We live on a corner and our breakfast nook has a window on each side. As we watch the children passing by we especially notice the ones who are going to school earlier than the rest. Three little boys walk by about seven-twenty, to reach school in time for breakfast, which the school furnishes. In winter, it is still dark when the boys pass. Next is a frail little boy trudging alone, also to get there in time for breakfast. The mothers of such children probably leave home before or when the children do.

Like the mothers of James and John, most mothers ask little for themselves. That is typical.

If we love our mothers we want to show them our love in many ways. Here are three suggestions: (1) Tell her that you love and appreciate her. (2) Try to be worthy of the price your mother paid in giving you life and support. (3) Try more than just *doing* something; also *be* something.

Mother

Oh, what a rich and blessed word!
So dear, so precious, and so mild!
'Twas from her lips that oft I heard
Such loving guidance for her child.

She was so fine and dear to me;
    She taught me as she watched me grow.
She prayed each day that I might see
    The path which God would have me go.

In each success, she would rejoice;
    When failure came, she truly cared.
She taught that I should make my choice
    For right, in spite of dangers dared.

Mother and Wife

The one who gave my children birth,
    Who blessed my world, and taught them well;
Whose faithful life brought love and mirth,
    And from whose lips words of wisdom fell.

Mothers!

Sweet girls who bore those precious grands;
    And dear sweet grands who mother greats;
Yes, mothers are the blessed strands
    Which seek to guide to heaven's gates.

                             J. T. Bolding

22
Today's Blessings
(Thanksgiving)

It is a good thing to give thanks unto the Lord, and to sing praises unto thy name, O most High (Ps. 92:1).

If ye abide in me, and my words abide in you, ye shall ask what ye will, and it shall be done unto you (John 15:7).

At a church meeting some women were naming things for which they were thankful. After new cars, new homes, or new furniture were mentioned, a frail little woman read the following poem which she had clipped out of a farm magazine. The poem reflected her attitude on life.

For These

Clean clothes I hung on the line,
    Pride in an old hat I trimmed,
Small tracks I mopped off the floor,
    A little dress that I hemmed,
Seeds I sowed in warm earth,
    Food I bought at the store,
Rooms I straightened with pride,
    My husband's step at the door,
Pies I baked for a friend,
    Blue jeans I patched at the knee,
Bedtime stories I told,
    Red yarn I knit tranquilly,

The letter I took time to write,
  Tears that "go-away" at my touch,
For today's blessings,
    Dear God
  I humbly thank you—so much!

Unknown

That little rhyme expresses a truly thankful heart. Luxuries of life are great, but they cannot fill an empty heart. They cannot give the joy we feel when we have helped others.

In the Book of Deuteronomy we read that the Israelites were reminded of all the blessings God had given them during their forty nomadic years in the wilderness. After the blessings were listed, they were admonished to be grateful.

As we come to Thanksgiving Day it is well for us to remember our experiences over the past years and to be grateful for God's care. Gratitude is one of the most beautiful graces a person can have, but the grace of gratitude must be learned just as the art of giving.

When both my husband and I were in school at the seminary, my husband was also the pastor of two country churches. Our three children were small, and we were on a tight budget. The people in those churches, however, were very good to us, frequently giving us canned fruits and vegetables. Since we didn't have much materially, every gift was a blessing.

One day we were having lunch at the home of one of these church families. After we ate, as the children played, one of the men called our little boy to him and gave him two nickels (a nickel would buy a candy bar in those days).

Our son was so happy with his gift that he ran to show it to me and then to his father. But my husband told him to return the money.

At that moment my husband forgot the grace of gratitude. Our son was broken-hearted, the man who gave him the nickel was embarrassed, and no good was served by my husband's pride. My husband was young and new as a pastor and he thought that our son asked for the nickel. He wanted to teach his child a lesson about maintaining pride by not accepting charity. But my husband forgot about the many gifts of fruits and vegetables our family received.

God pours out blessings upon us every day. Be grateful and happy with them. Along with feeling grateful, be humble before God and face Thanksgiving Day with contrite hearts. Think of mistakes you have made. Ask God to forgive you.

God gives some blessings to each of us. These blessings vary. We should realize God knows what each of us needs and gives to us accordingly. Don't compare your situations with others. That's what Shirley did. She was six years old and her playmate Billy was six months younger. When Billy's birthday came he rushed to Shirley's house and said, "Now I am six years old, too."

Shirley thought a moment and then replied, "Yes, but I am more sixer than you are."

In our pride we often quibble over being "sixer" than our friend or neighbor. We often guess wrongly that other people have either more or less than we do.

To be truly thankful at Thanksgiving time, remember the blessings of the past. Think of times when someone near and dear to you was sick. God answered your prayer and that person was healed. Think of the times when you experienced even small blessings. It may have been when you lost something. After you prayed and asked God to help you find it, you went right to the place where it had been left. This book could not hold all the memories of blessings sent from God.

Along with past blessings, be grateful for our present blessings. Rejoice that our lives right now are good. A few months ago our pastor asked our prayer group to pray for an unemployed man and his family, that work would be found. A week or two later he asked us to pray for them again. The family was suffering since no job had opened up. People continued to pray for the family. Then on another Wednesday night, the pastor told us he had just received a phone call from the mother of this family. Her husband had just gotten a job that day. She wanted our church to know how grateful and happy they were.

Also, we can be happier at Thanksgiving if our relationships with others are harmonious. During five months after school started this year, we watched two little sisters walk by on their way to school. They obviously enjoyed each other. Our breakfast just tasted better as we saw the girls often holding hands, sometimes singing. What a blessing it is to be right with God and right with each other.

Not only at Thanksgiving but all through the year we should be grateful. Gratitude is a key to positive, happy relationships. In marriage, gratitude is an ingredient for success. For example, one husband and wife frequently seem to be cross with each other whereas another couple seem to be mostly happy with each other. What makes the difference? If you could study those couples closely, you likely will find that unhappy couples are constantly wanting more. They seldom feel they have all they are due. If the husband buys his wife a gift, she thinks it should have been better. Such couples are not aware of the blessings they already have.

Happy the couples when husband and wife appreciate each other. They thank each other. They graciously accept favors and courtesies from each other. They are content with each other and with what they have. Does that quality of gratitude characterize your relationship all year long?

It's time to be thankful. Be thankful for the home you share with your precious family. Be grateful for the church home you share with your spiritual brothers and sisters. Most of all, thank God for the eternal home He is preparing for you.

Thanksgiving

Thanksgiving time is here again,
    And all our hearts agree
That formal thanks rise from our land
    For fruits of God's "blessing tree."

For freedom, health, for life and fresh air,
    For loved ones, homes, and peace of mind;
For work through which we earn daily bread;
    For friendships—precious ties that bind.

With grateful hearts, we come dear Lord,
    On this day and all other days,
In joyful song and with happy thanks,
    To raise our voice in grateful praise.

J. T. Bolding

23
Christmas

And the angel said unto them, Fear not: for, behold, I bring you good tidings of great joy, which shall be to all people. For unto you is born this day in the city of David a Saviour, which is Christ the Lord   (Luke 2:10, 11).

And suddenly there was with the angel a multitude of heavenly host praising God, and saying, Glory to God in the highest, and on earth peace, good will toward men   (Luke 2;13, 14).

What does Christmas mean to you?

A man in a prison camp became so discouraged at Christmas time that he decided to end his life if only he could find a way. His bare, cold room offered no means for suicide.

Waking from a restless sleep he thought of the Christmas times in his past. As a child his family would sing the carols they had learned at school and church. He smiled weakly as he remembered the church pageant. He had been a small wise man and his sister had been an even smaller angel. As he remembered, he started to hum softly,

> Away in a manger, no crib for his bed,
> The little Lord Jesus lay down his sweet head.

Through the rest of the night he sang or hummed snatches of songs he could remember. The words and tunes gave him new hope and courage.

What does Christmas mean to you? Is your heart filled with hope and courage?

Aaron was a middle-aged man who worked as a laborer and was willing to do all kinds of odd jobs in his small town, many times taking on tasks others refused to do. He had built his own little shack of a house. He was cheerful and never lacked for work.

Aaron loved Christmas. Although he received very few presents in his life, he saved all year so he could give to others on Christmas.

Early Christmas morning he would take small gifts to poor families. Then, with packages of peppermint candy, he would go to the homes of old people who had no one to bring them gifts.

All day long he went about cheering people. When it was dark he would return to his little house and sit by the fire. As he rocked, he would say to himself, "Wasn't this one of my best Christmases?" He knew the great gift that comes from making others happy.

What ways are you planning to make others happier this Christmas season? What does Christmas mean to you?

One cold, stormy night near Christmas, Joel and Ethel sat in their beautiful home. She had finished decorating the house. Everything looked just right for the holidays.

They sat reading, but there as a cold feeling between them. Little love had been in their home for a number of years. They had blamed each other when their only child, a boy, had been killed in a car wreck.

As Ethel looked at the beautiful tree, she thought how much she would like their child to be there with them to enjoy it. As Joe tried to ignore the decorations he thought of a man who worked for him. The man made a small salary, his family was large, and his wife had been sick.

"Isn't this the night the stores stay open late?" he asked.

"Yes, but the mall is very crowded," Ethel replied.

"Well, get your hat and coat, we're going to buy some gifts." Joe got up and began to put on his coat and gloves.

Ethel didn't want to go out into the cold, but, on the other hand, Joe had not asked her to go anyplace for many months.

Soon they were holding hands as they looked at clothes for children. They bought so much that they had to go to the car several times and unload their packages.

Later, they shopped at the grocery store. "Buy what you would buy if our boy was still with us," Joe suggested. When they finished with the shopping they drove across town to the home of the man who worked for Joe.

"Why, Mr. Joe, is something wrong?" the man asked when he opened the door.

"No, everything is all right. But we can't have a real party at our house because we lost our child. So we're bringing a party over here to you."

Soon the children were carrying packages and groceries into the house. Ethel helped cook some of the food they had bought. Joe smiled as he watched the presents of clothes and some toys being opened by the children. It was nearly twelve o'clock when Joe and Ethel returned to their home.

"Joe," Ethel said when they had hung up their coats. "I had forgotten what love is. Tonight you made me see that love lives on forever."

Joe put his arms around Ethel and said, "I had decided I could not go on and planned to leave you and this house after Christmas. But something kept saying, 'get out and make someone happy.'"

Joe and Ethel started a new tradition of taking a Christmas party to some needy family each year. They were happy again. They began talking openly to each other about their child, and how much they had loved him. Talking about him made him seem near again.

What does Christmas mean to you?

Beyond the giving of presents, are you sharing anything of yourself with someone this season?

We think of tidings of joy especially at Christmas. But life goes on whatever the season, and many around us have heavy hearts. We know what the tidings of joy are all about. Let's bring the message to others.

Along with glad tidings of joy are tidings of peace. People like Joe and Ethel need peace. We have the way of peace in our hearts if we have given them to Jesus. Have you shared the true way to peace with others?

There is a reward for those who bring good tidings. "How beautiful are the feet of them that preach the gospel of peace, and bring glad tidings of good things!" (Rom. 10:15).

We might not have much in this world. But all of us who know the Savior have the gifts of joy and peace to share with others.

> A cup of cold water, He'll not overlook,
>   If given as unto the Lord;
> How little it takes for the Savior to note,
>   And in glory to richly reward.
>
> Who cheerfully, willingly gives to the Lord,
>   His promise of blessing is sure;
> That He will provide an abundant reward,
>   Through eternity it will endure.
>
> Selected

24

Guidelines for Growth
New Year

Gather the people together, men, and women, and children . . . that they may hear, and that they may learn . . . and observe to do all the words of this law   (Deut. 31:12).

People who buy antiques expect them to increase in value a little more each year they are kept. A family in Pennsylvania owns a valuable and treasured clock. It is a grandfather clock, which they claim was made in Zug, Switzerland, about four hundred years ago. Not only is it very old, but it still ticks.

The clock keeps ticking because the owners have kept it in good repair. The present owner has a record showing that the clock was repaired in 1803, after the family who owned it at that time moved it from Europe to America.

All of us need to pause during this New Year's celebration to see if we need to make repairs as we move from the old year into the new.

We are God's possession, and He expects us to grow a little more each year in a useful and spiritual way.

Looking back, have you been in God's house to worship each week? The scripture above states that the people were gathered together. If you need improvement in this practice, make as one of your new guidelines for the next year the resolve to gather with God's people every Sunday.

How are your private devotions and Bible reading going lately? Have these become a steady practice each day?

"Come now, and let us reason together, saith the Lord" (Isa. 1:18). How can we reason together without studying the Bible? Therefore, a second guideline for the new year is the practice to study the Bible more effectively and perhaps more frequently.

The psalmist said, "Thy word have I hid in mine heart, that I might not sin against thee" (Ps. 119:11). Study God's Word—at home and with God's people

We can be happier Christians by meeting together each week in our places of worship—to praise God, to study his Word, and to grow as Christians. But is there more? Absorbing God's Word is well and good, but even this can become spiritually unhealthy if we do not share what we have taken in.

It's likely we all can do more to share our faith with others in the coming year. The Bible says, "Go out into the highways and hedges, and compel them to come in, that my house may be filled" (Luke 14:23).

We may regularly assemble for worship and faithfully study His Word, but we also have a commission to seek out those who are lost and invite them to come with us to worship.

At certain times of the year football coaches from the universities go out to high schools and observe outstanding players. They invite those special players to come to their schools. They not only invite; they plead; they offer scholarships; they try to woo those players.

Jesus wants us to personally invite the lost and unenlisted to come to His house and receive His salvation. What would happen if we would recruit the way football coaches do? We can start by sensing the urgent needs of people around us.

Of Jesus, the gospel writer said, "But when he saw the multitudes, he was moved with compassion on them, because they fainted, and were scattered abroad, as sheep having no shepherd" (Matt. 9:36). Our vision to reach the lost should touch our neighborhoods and our places of work. Together our vision can touch the whole world.

Do you have compassion for a world filled with a helpless, and hungry humanity urgently needing our attention for both physical and spiritual needs?

When a report came that a plane carrying a family of four had gone down on a mountain in Colorado, teams of rescuers went out to search. They had no success and became very cold and tired. But they kept on searching because they had hearts filled with compassion for the people who had gone down with that plane.

After a few days the plane was spotted from the air, and rescue workers were able to get to the wreckage. The parents were dead, but the two children were still alive. They were rushed to a hospital.

What if the rangers had said: "It is too expensive to send a helicopter; we can't be bothered!" Those two children would have died slowly from starvation and injuries.

Are we willing to expend more money, prayer, and talent to search out those who need God? Has our support of missions grown cold?

Another guideline for the new year is an active practice of prayer. How is your individual prayer life? Are you also praying with other Christians? Are you talking candidly to God and waiting for answers?

Isn't it wonderful to be alive and to face a new year?
For all the blessings of the year,
For all the friends we hold so dear
For peace on earth, both far and near,
We thank Thee, Lord.

We have focused on some guidelines for living this coming year. Resolve, with God's help, to practice each of them more faithfully and productively.

Have a good year!